Seesaw

Quirky Poems

Ken Tomaro and Nolcha Fox

Seesaw

ISBN: 978-1-962374-43-9 Paperback
ISBN: 978-1-962374-44-6 Epub

Permissions have been granted and filed by the publisher.
Publisher: Prolific Pulse Press LLC
Prolificpulse.com admin@prolificpulse.com

Published April 2025 Raleigh, North Carolina USA

Seesaw

Seesaw

Introduction

Ken and Nolcha met in the Thursday Night Poets group. Their writing relationship began when their similar quirky sense of dark humor led them to write poems based on a word or phrase in each other's poetry. To maintain sanity and remind themselves that writing poetry is fun, they decided to write collaboratively. And that's how this book came about.

Nolcha's stanzas are right-aligned, Ken's are left-aligned.

Thanks to these literary magazines for publishing some of the poems in this collection.

- *Lothlorien Poetry Journal*: "I come to a door," "If you want it bad enough," "Trees hide"
- *MasticadoresUSA*: "Chimes"
- *Medusa's Kitchen*: "Sharp Words," "Dude, My Hands Are Huge!" "God Drops the Ball Again," "In my dreams," "The flu," "Victory is wearing," "You stand on the brim"
- *Roi Faineant Press*: "I was driving into the sun," "King Cake," "The Soundtrack to My Life"
- *Yorick Radio Productions Podcast*: "As surely as," "Debris that hurries by"

All I Can Think of Is Food

The mold loves the damp
in this out-of-the-way dump,
but it's worth the extra mile
since the food is cooked with mole.

I invite all my friends,
the cats, the rats, opossums,
and skunks
to my little trash dump party.
It's a casual, relaxed affair.

All my little furry friends
refuse to dine
at any dump but mine.
They raid the fridge
for beer and snacks,
and they don't mind
the moldy food.
If they would only
clean the house,
I'd let them stay
forever.

Have a seat.
Enjoy the moonlight view.
It's especially pretty tonight,
compost steam
rising in the tepid air.

Seesaw

Oh, look, leftover ribs!
And crunchy rice!
They pair well
with the last bit of
cream of mushroom soup
clinging to the ridges
of the can.

Being single has its perks,
to go and do without a care,
But eating out in my backyard
by compost heap makes my
nostrils cringe.
Leftovers and canned
delights somersault my gut.
It's time to find a willing mate
who likes to cook and clean.
Or go back home to mom.

Being single has its perks.
I can eat moldy food
without a care,
or cold soup from a can.
No one around to compliment
the odorous bouquet filling the air.
Just don't tell my mom.
I don't want her to worry.
And I certainly don't want
to go back home.

Seesaw

Neighbors called the County.
Now hazmat workers fill my house.
That's one way to clean it up.
I don't have to go home to mom.
What can I eat for dinner?

Apathy

I haven't washed the sheets in weeks.
The sink is full of crusted dishes.
My hair is home to rats and bugs.
I don't care if I'm a slob.
The flies will clean the place for me,
and they work for breadcrumbs.
I slouch on the couch,
a slab of apathy
sandwiched between the pillows.

And now I want a sandwich,
but it won't make itself.
Maybe I can train the rats
how to cook.
But that takes work.
And who has time for all that?
Maybe I could...
maybe I could...
Eh, starving is fine.

Starving is fine
until I can't hear the TV
over tummy rumbles
and grumbles.
Maybe I can order out.
If I can find my wallet.

Seesaw

Rats! My wallet is full of
bugs and cobwebs.
Are those crumbs in the carpet?
I hope no one sees me
eating carpet crumbs.
Perhaps I'll fall asleep
dreaming my unwashed pillows
are dirty marshmallows.
But dreaming takes work.

I'm glad I closed the curtains
before I scarfed up those crumbs
(and accidentally
vacuumed the carpet).
My nosy niece would report
me to the police
for lewd and indecent behavior.
I may crash on the couch.
Getting into PJs is too much work.

Oh, the agony
of just the thought
of considering moving
even so much as my big toe.
I'm just going to float here
in this empty space,
a giant, naked, amoeba.
Blob of blobs.
To my nosy niece
and the police,
I would apologize for
my nakedness,

but my apathy prevents me.
Meh, I'm sure to get where I'm going.
Words and words and words.

I get I'm not getting anywhere.
Even the flies are appalled.
They like to eat what doesn't move,
but they think I might bite.

I'll pretend they taste like raisins.
But that...takes...work.
If only my mother
could see me now.
There is a fine line between
apathetic and plain old pathetic,
but I lack the empathy to care.

Empathy is too much work.
So is caring if
I'm pathetic.
Isn't that pathetic?

Why am I so hard on myself?
That's it, today's the day!
I'm going to write a book called
On Being Sympathetic
to the Apathetic Empath.
Oh, who am I kidding?
That takes work.

Seesaw

As surely as

Godzilla stomps on Tokyo,
gravity will crush my bones.
My boobs will try to kiss my knees.
My gut will contemplate the floor.
I'll need some steps to reach the shelves.
Gravity is not my friend.

Gravity makes things move
in most peculiar ways–
like the spare tire
hovering over my belt.
My eyelids will droop
as the world goes dark.

As surely as

The Hulk will SMASH
my unmentionables
shall never be mentioned again.
Gravity, why can't we be friends?

Gravity, I need a lift.
Don't make me fall
from places high, like planes.
to places low, like graves.
Can't you give me one more break,
And let me float awhile?

Seesaw

Bits and pieces of me,
things floating haphazardly
that shouldn't float at all.
Gravity, can you...
Oh, never mind.
At this rate, eventually
I'll be able to kiss my own ass.

Chimes

Winds hurl chimes against the window.
Shattered fragments cut our losses,
bleeding time, condemning us to pain.

It is dark where I stand.
But I can see off in the distance, a field.
I can make out a low fog.
There is no wind, no sound.

I cannot hear the wind.
I see its path.
Leaves and birds chime hello
as they brush against
the sun.

In the early morning,
the fog has lifted.
The field I could barely see
the night before
flows like a river melting to the horizon.
The birds and a gentle breeze
nudge the sun awake, but not for long.

The sun awakes
and melts the fog.
The fields are rivers of green
rippling in the wind.

Seesaw

Wind, sun, fog,
the birds in a towering evergreen,
fields of grass
come together,
a seamless orchestra,
a sunlit sonata.

Windchimes the music
for sunlit sonatas,
accompanying birdsong
in flight.

Debris that hurries by

becomes a melody and why
aren't we taking cover
instead of videoing
this hurricane
on our phones?

Aluminum siding
and a trampoline whiz by.
So, I'll snap a pic
for all the wandering eyes,
just to break the monotony
of cat photos
on my phone.

Whoa, there goes the cat
with a bird in its mouth,
still flapping!
I fly close behind
shooting photos
and posting on Facebook.
Til the wind grabs
my phone from my hand.

It's true what they say-
a cat always lands on its feet,
even with a mouthful of bird.
But you'll never know,
since the cat, like my camera,
is gone with the wind.

Dude, My Hands Are Huge!

That explains so much!
Somewhere in my childhood,
I inhaled too many fumes
from Super Elastic Bubble Plastic.
It's all so clear, or not so.

I'm stuck in traffic.
Inching forward,
going nowhere slow,
inhaling toxic fumes
belched out the back
of vehicles around me.
The fumes melt into
toxic smog that blurs the sun
and eats my lungs.
I do this for a living.
Or maybe it's a dying.

My life is anything but super.
My waistline, the only thing elastic.
I live in my own little bubble,
surrounded by people made of plastic.
I can't remember if I locked the door,
zipped my pants,
watered the plants, took out the trash.
Yes, I think this is dying.

Seesaw

Plastic elastic trash
fills the house.
Tables, chairs, bags,
combs, spoons, plants
I never water.
I don't ever lock my house.
It's filled with Super
Elastic Bubble Plastic
that no one wants to steal.

Ghosts glimmer

in moonlight, sob words
from the poems I buried
in the garden, under roses.

My tears nourish
these buried poems,
still very much alive,
a touch of new soil.

My words are soiled,
undernourished,
as wilted as the roses
In my garden.

My words, only ghosts
of what used to be,
wandering the landscape
of this poetic garden.

Seesaw

God Drops the Ball Again

Everyone tells me I'm doing God's work.
And all I can think is,
God needs to get off his ass
and start chipping in.

> I need to get off my ass
> and do God's work.
> But coffee is calling.
> Wait, what was I thinking about?

God! This work is hard!
And my ass hurts from sitting on it.
And the coffee won't stop calling.
And a woman's work is never done.
And I'm not even a woman.
Wait, what was I thinking about?

> My thoughts are scrambling
> for the exit, tired of sitting
> on their asses, praying
> for the weekend. Or a nap.
> Praise be God for coffee beans,
> a grand excuse to drink
> caffeine and get away from work.

Seesaw

Sometimes you have to put work aside,
God's or otherwise.
Sit back with a plate of scrambled thoughts,
a side of toast, drum of coffee,
and just sit on your ass.
Maybe say a prayer to God, or otherwise.

God is way bigger than my ass.
That's comforting to know.

Seesaw

He is a house

at the end of the road,
lost love parting curtains
of his eyes. She peers
into empty gardens,
fades into dark corners,
pauses at landings,
treads splintered stairs,
sits on faded couches,
feet on threadbare carpets,
waiting for him
to turn on the lights.

The road is a dead-end,
curtains worn and brittle.
She peers through
a tangle of overgrown weeds,
pauses at fallen corners,
a staircase now in pieces,
envisions the old couch,
orange shag carpet,
remembering him.
The lights are on
but it's no longer a home.

She calls for him,
the only sound
an echo of his name.

Seesaw

She whispers for him,
an echo of his name
that no longer
makes a sound.

                    She turns off the lights
                       and closes the door.
           This house isn't hers anymore.
                        One last look back
                   in search of his shadow.
                      Nothing. He's gone.
                              She leaves.

How to Use an Inner Tube

I cling to an old inner tube
as white water tosses me
down this river.
Inner tubes are the latest rage.
That's what these torrents say.

I wait patiently
for the current to calm,
so that I might enjoy
a lazy day.
Although the rubber
in the hot sun
burns my ass a little.
And that is my latest rage.

Inner tubes hang
around my car
protecting my new paint job,
when other drivers
plow through traffic
in a fit of road rage.

The tubes in my inner ear
vibrate violently,
ringing
ringing
ringing,
a traffic jam of cars
rumbling through
an otherwise hollow tunnel
in a mental fit of road rage.

I come to a door

I open it.
Not because it's easy,
or because I'm curious,
or because I'm bored,
but because it is the only one
that will open.
I take weak little steps.
Not because I am unsure,
but because I am tired.
I follow the same path.
Not because it is worn,
but because all paths are the same.

The only door that opens
is to dirty dishes, unmade beds,
laundry someone left behind.
By the time I clean this house,
I'll be too weak
to find a pathway out of here.

So, I walk through the door,
do the dishes and laundry,
clean the house.
I pay a few bills to keep the lights on,
hoping to brighten the path,
that someone may find me.

Seesaw

I close the door
and turn off the lights
so that no one can find me.
Maybe they'll stop
sending bills.

Return to sender:
Recipient no longer at this address.

Seesaw

I sat along the banks

of my stream of consciousness
to see if the words were flowing.

My words are flowing down the drain.
If I turn on the garbage disposal,
nobody will know they ever were.

The words swirled around in circles before
smashing against the bottom-feeding rocks,
catching in the branches of a fallen tree,
before flowing broken into the mouth
of a great lake.

If I swallow my words,
sucking them back into my mouth,
will my head explode?

I dove headfirst into the lake,
gulping up water by the mouthful,
hoping to swallow these broken words,
hoping to start over fresh.
And it was too late
before I realized it was no great lake at all,
but nature's festering toilet.
And my words and I were swirling helplessly
around the bowl
into the murky abyss.

Seesaw

I spit my words into nature's festering toilet,
watch them swirl around the bowl,
then clean my mouth with soap.

I was driving into the sun

Queen and Bowie singing on the radio,
the universe in chaos.
Sun shining, snow falling,
cars honking and swerving.
A man, or a woman,
or whatever image you choose,
rode down from heaven on a white horse.

I was driving into the sun
wearing my darkest shades.
I couldn't hear the radio
for the wind. I honked
and swerved past idiots
with eyes fixed on their cell phones.
I hope for help from heaven
before we all crash and die.

I was driving into the sun.
And before I could touch the surface,
I collided with a white horse
riding down from heaven.
And like the Big Bang,
I became part of the chaos in the universe
and heard everything.

Seesaw

I was riding into the sun
on a white horse wearing shades
(both of us, that is)
up the stairway to heaven,
to escape the chaos and find
the meaning of life.

I was riding into the sun.
Me, on a white horse
gliding up the stairway to heaven,
when I realized
Chaos IS the meaning of life.
And the shades covering our eyes
hid nothing.

If you want it bad enough,

it's your toothpaste.
Get up every day
and brush your teeth.

It's your coffee.
Drink a cup or two,
and let the subtle roast
work its magic.

Give up everything
you want for Lent.
Except coffee.
Never give up coffee.

Or just give up.

Just kidding!
Just making sure you're awake.
If you want it bad enough,
never give up,

unless you're treading water
in the middle of the ocean,
miles away from land.

All the coffee in the world
won't help.

Seesaw

My alarm dog
won't bring coffee.
I don't know if she swims.
Don't go in the ocean.
And don't give up caffeine.

Screw it, just give up!
Sink to the ocean bottom.
Invite the fish
for a cup of coffee.
Don't worry about the alarm...
the dog will get it.

King Cake

We received a king cake at the office the other day,
part coffee cake, part cinnamon roll,
bathed in an icing of yellow, green, and purple.
A Mardi Gras rainbow.
Inside the cake hides a small plastic baby.
And, depending on your view, either marks the arrival of the three wise men or symbolizes luck and prosperity.
But I have questions, as always.
How does the plastic not melt in the baking process?
How lucky can you consider yourself after biting into a plastic baby?

She was always losing things.
The eraser end of a pencil
floated in her nostril, it jiggled
when she sneezed, but she
could never find it.
Her keys were somewhere
in that purse that she left
in the taxi.
And the baby, where
was that baby?

Makeover

After therapy to deal with
feeling unwanted,
the Grim Reaper auctioned
his robe and scythe
through Sotheby's,
learned karaoke
and how to chat.

Now you can meet him
at Starbucks, bars,
and parties.
He's in pinstripe
and dark glasses.

He aims to give you
what you want.
Free drinks on the house,
your drugs of choice,
limos to Vegas,
just name your vice.

They prescribed him the latest pills.
It's easier to hide
the unanswered questions
than to confront them.
New clothes don't make a new man.

Seesaw

The pinstripes, his prison.
He became the death of the party,
hiding in the dark corners.
He claims to give you
anything you want,
but nothing of what you need,
and gives up on therapy altogether.

Secret Wishes Seen Together

My pen starts my day with a morality play.
Joy is a con artist.
"Everything is going to be amazing."
Counting and not counting
secret wishes seen together.
What if something scary flails?
Spring flowers are time unfolding,
as I dance the walking pneumonia stomp.

It's an off, off, off-Broadway
kind of show.
Everything was going amazingly
until everyone broke a leg.
Now I'm counting the minutes
until the curtain falls,
and I hobble offstage
on broken dreams
and broken bones.

I wheeze and hobble off stage right
before the curtain falls,
to see the doc, to set my bones,
and tourniquet my dreams.
Secret wishes ground to dust,
no money in my pocket.
The only thing amazing
is that I am still alive.

Seesaw

The reviews are in.
Five stars from that one guy
who lived in that place,
who also raved
about a cheeseburger once.
And being alive,
I have no time to waste.
The sequel,
a guaranteed blockbuster.
Did I say right?
I should say, exit stage left.

Seesaw

The flu

blows out my spark,
removes some bone,
bores out a space inside my chest,
and fills the void with phlegm.

Every cough, every heaving
of my wet lungs,
I share a small piece of me
with the world.

Sharing is caring.
I fill the air with drops
of phlegm so
you'll remember me.

But then,
how could you ever
forget me?
These little drops of phlegm
cover the sky like a million stars.
Did you know a million stars
is called a spittle?
How could you forget me now?

The Soundtrack to My Life

Here comes your debaser man
to hang on your cross
in the Jesus Christ pose.
Don't save it for later, just
hammer another nail in my heart.
It's a wave of mutilation.
What a fucking lovely day
in a beautiful world.

You're under pressure, Annie Hopparen.
Get your gun. Remember,
distance equals rate times time.
Goodbye, Gemini girl,
go wild in the country.
Stand and deliver a swingin' safari.

You are a pixie
standing in a garden of sound,
drumming to an English beat.
Slayer of queens.
A blazing arrow.
You are Adam, bowing to the Garden of Eden,
in sweet soul limbo, dancing with ants.
You are you.
And you are music to my ears.

Ken's playlist:
- Bert Kaempfert: "A Swingin' Safari"
- Stephen Merritt: "What a Fucking Lovely Day"
- Slayer: "Gemini"
- Pixies: Wave of Mutilation," "Here Comes Your Man," "Debaser," "Distance Equals Rate Times Time"
- Colin Hay: "Beautiful World"
- Bow Wow Wow: "Go Wild in the Country"
- Chateau Neuf: "Hopparen"
- Adam and the Ants: "Stand and Deliver"
- Soundgarden: "Jesus Christ Pose"
- Squeeze: "Annie Get Your Gun," "Another Nail in My Heart," "Goodbye Girl"
- Booker T. & the MG's: "Soul Limbo"
- Blackalicious: "Blazing Arrow"
- English Beat: "Save it for Later"
- Queen & Bowie: "Under Pressure"

This river

is a rocky road,
rippling diamonds
with each footstep.
Catch petal confetti
tossed by breezes,
singing "Welcome back."
Listen to the locomotive
calling cedar waxwings
to return to roost.
Smell the splash
of childhood laughter
bouncing off
the metal bridge.

This river,
a winding path
whose destiny
was chosen by the wind.
A crystal chandelier, reflections
scattering in the sunlight.
Listen to the locomotive
calling for home again.
Dive into the waves
of childhood laughter
echoing from the metal bridge.

Childhood jumps off the bridge
to splash in sunlit river water,
spraying old age with crystal
chandelier reflections.

Seesaw

This river
is a lifeboat
so that we may follow its path
to a greater destiny.

Too Blue

Blue swings in the park, feet touching the sky.
Blue finds a quarter while prowling the street.
Blue paints my veins, my toenails, too.
Blue drinks the moonlight and swallows the sun.
Blue shakes the leaves of the cottonwood tree.
Blue plays the sax on the overpass bridge.
Blue swigs some suds at an old, sleazy bar.
Blue paints the town, then hides in my eyes.

Brown is the dirt,
when my feet touch the ground.
Silver is the quarter left in the street.
Plum and hot pink
is the blood in my veins.
Umber, the color of the cottonwood tree.
Green are the leaves,
not just the ones you can see.
Brass is the notes
from the sax on the bridge.
A rainbow of cocktails
while drinking with friends.
The world is a painting
through kaleidoscope eyes.
Blue is the sadness
when we say our goodbyes.

Trees hide

my plans for the future.
Leaves cover memory
of where I began.
I cannot go forward,
I cannot return.
Branches block moonlight
and shroud me in shadows.
I'm lost to myself
and the ghosts that I love.

Gray bark covers the scars,
shading my brittle skin
from the heat of the sun.
Lost are the memories
of where we all began.
I cannot go forward,
I cannot return.
Love is lost in the trees,
ghosts hiding in the moonlight.

My skin is scarred
and brittle
from love lost
in the trees.
The sun melts
paths to past regrets.
The shadows
shroud the future.

Seesaw

Past and future,
like the branches of a tree
lead to different paths,
sometimes the same regrets.

Seesaw

Victory is wearing

> your enemy's head
> to dinner.

Victory is convincing the world
you are harmless,
and knowing otherwise.

> A deer, a deer,
> A gentle deer,
> or is Bambi really
> Godzilla?

But even Godzilla
had a gentle side.
He only did
what he had to do.

> Maybe we're all monsters
> with a frosting of sweet
> to cover the poison.

———

Inspired by Cowboy State Daily

Where the Wild Goose Goes

When the fog lifts
mournful honking
to the twilight,
I stop and drop a dish.
I want to grow some feathers,
fly away from mundane life.
Let me follow, follow
where the wild goose goes.

Into the wild white clouds,
I will follow.
Cool, dense fog
between my feathers.
In the early, first light
of morning,
I will follow,
follow you from
this mundane life.

My feather boa
wants to fly.
I must follow
as it sails in the wind.
Dressing sexy
to avoid the mundane
is more work
than I thought it would be.

Seesaw

Words don't fail me

Words don't disappoint or judge.
Words cannot hurt me,
Only the person who speaks them.

Sharp words
slice the sunlight
into little
pats of butter.

Seesaw

You stand on the brim

of your ambitions,
a well with no bottom
in sight. Peer into
murky moonlit reflection,
what do you see staring back?

I'll tell you what I see. I see me,
skin rippling in the moonlight.
Ripples, wrinkles, potato, potahto.
What am I supposed to see
in the eternity of a bottomless well?
I see all those things others cannot.

What things do you see
that others cannot?
In rippled reflection,
do you shake hands
with the you
in the shadows?

Maybe I was wrong.
Maybe they were the things
I *didn't* want to see.
I reach for my own hand down in this well.
But being bottomless, endless,
it was a handshake never connected.

Author Bios

Never until recently did he consider writing poetry. Not when he slid from the womb. Not when he felt the first tingle of teen hormones. Not after he got married, divorced, moved to another city, lost a couple jobs, moved back. It just sort of happened. **Ken Tomaro**, self-proclaimed poet laureate of the Cleveland sewer system, has been writing poetry for a few short years.

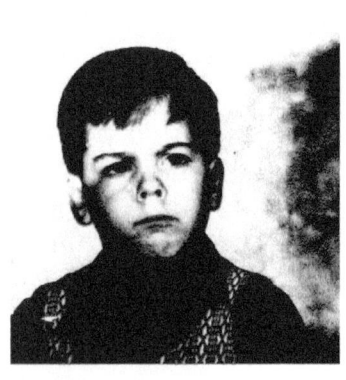

He's not famous, rich, recognized or read in schools across America. He has been published in several literary journals, done a couple podcasts, started the YouTube channel, Screaming Down the Poetic Highway, and that's pretty damn impressive. KenTomaro.com

Seesaw

Nolcha Fox's poems have been curated in print and online journals. Her poetry books are available on Amazon and Dancing Girl Press. **Nominee for 2023, 2024, and 2025 Best of The Net. Nominee for 2023 and 2024 Pushcart Prize. Editor of** Chewers by Masticadores. **Co-Poetry Editor of LatinosUSA.**

Websites: https://bit.ly/3bT9tYu and https://nolchafox2.wixsite.com/nolcha-s-written-wor/blog
Facebook: facebook.com/nolcha.fox/

www.ingramcontent.com/pod-product-compliance
Lightning Source LLC
Chambersburg PA
CBHW021005150626
46549CB00012BA/1290